Stuck in the Middle:

The Mistakes That Jeopardize Your Financial Success and How to Fix Them

Dan Danford, CFP®

Stuck in the Middle

ISBN 978-1506-903-24-8 HC/DJ
ISBN 978-1506-903-23-1 PRINT
ISBN 978-1506-903-25-5 EBOOK

LCCN 2016956353

October 2016

Published and Distributed by
First Edition Design Publishing, Inc.
P.O. Box 20217, Sarasota, FL 34276-3217
www.firsteditiondesignpublishing.com

TABLE OF CONTENTS

Introduction

I've spoken to a lot of people about investing and finances over the years. My first stint in the business was as a trust officer for a regional bank in 1984. My area of responsibility was tax-qualified retirement plans and Individual Retirement Accounts. Since then, I've visited with thousands of people planning for or living in retirement.

Of course, the nature of my business puts me in contact with people who are serious about retirement. They wouldn't be talking with an investment advisor if they weren't saving, investing, and anticipating some retirement fruits from their labors. Mostly, they have the basics right. Nearly all of them are sincere and most are on the right track.

I'm often surprised, however, at some of the financial mistakes I encounter. I don't mean things like math errors or misplaced credit cards, but rather ideas that conflict with what we know to be true today. Many people don't keep up with innovations in investing and so they are left with outdated information.

Another issue is where people learned their outdated lessons. A lot of basic money ideas come from early family experiences. Those early imprints are powerful and not easily changed, but the financial world of our parents was far different from the world today. Financial products, services, and fees were far different than they are today. It's a serious handicap to address today's challenges with yesterday's knowledge.

The most damaging mistakes typically arise from personal experience. Feelings and emotions about money are often strong — and wrong. Urges usually point the wrong way: the urge to sell when the market is down; the urge to buy when the market is up; the urge towards safety when volatility occurs; the urge towards tangible assets; the urge towards things we already know; the urge to save money by avoiding experts; the urge to follow the crowd. Most of these are rooted in psychology or sociology and for good reasons, but they point investors in the wrong direction for financial success.

That's really the point of this book. I'm hopeful that I can open your eyes to some better ways of doing things. Perhaps I can plant some seeds that will make your life journey more productive. Not every idea is for every person, but you and your advisor can consider the possibilities. Sometimes a modest change can add value, convenience, or performance to your investment efforts.

Performance gets outsize emphasis in most investment discussions and I get that. It is important, but in a long-term way that many people overlook. They get excited at the prospect of short-term gains and leap to mistakes that threaten longer-term results. I'll argue that many people get excited about performance mainly because it's the easiest metric to measure. Value and convenience are more subjective, and so harder to measure, but I contend that they are every bit as important to your success as pure performance.

The reason is because investment and financial issues are sideline considerations for most people who are too busy for deep research into investments. Their focus is typically on other issues: family, career, recreation, and meaningful relationships. Because of their attention to other areas, convenience and value are extremely helpful for a part-time pursuit of financial goals. Simply, if something isn't convenient or cost effective, it probably won't get done.

Finally, my goal is to introduce you to some new ideas that might explain some things you might not fully understand. This isn't a textbook and there are other great resources for deeper study. I simply want to share some ideas to help you succeed. I hope you and your advisor can explore these suggestions as they apply to your specific financial circumstances.

Chapter 1

Tax Refunds and Other Windfalls

Recently, a media reporter asked me for some suggestions for a story about tax refunds. She wanted some ideas as to what people might do with the money. It wasn't a new subject for me. Reporters often call when the lottery prize reaches the sky. I've probably done a half-dozen lottery interviews over the years and I try to offer some insights even though viewers or readers are unlikely to win. I typically make the same recommendations as I do for inheritances, bonuses, or other windfalls.

If you are the fortunate beneficiary of a windfall, I suggest that the money should satisfy your basic human instincts as well as accomplish some good. I believe people do best when they splurge a little and save a little. I suggest three destinations for the money:

Blow it. This is the fun part — the splurge. Take a weekend vacation or even a cruise if that appeals to you. Using some of the money to pursue pleasure is a piece of the American Dream…and the memories will bring you joy for years to come. We all need some joy in our lives. A lot of financial plans fail because they ignore the need for joy. Where's the joy in receiving a tax refund or bonus if it all goes toward paying off the credit cards or replacing the furnace?

Mow it. This is financial lawn maintenance. If you have a leaky roof, debts to pay, or need to establish a fund for emergencies, use some of the money to address issues that are holding you back. Enroll in a class if you suck at budgeting; order some software to track expenses or balance your checkbook. Few people succeed financially without occasionally mowing their financial lawn.

Grow it. An obvious choice is to reroute a chunk of the money into your retirement account or college funds. For maximum growth, plant seeds that can prosper over a decade or two. Jim Stowers, founder of the American Century family of mutual funds, once noted that the "perfect time to plant an oak tree was twenty years ago. The next perfect time is now."

But financial growth isn't the only option. In fact, it may not even be the best option. Perhaps a few college classes or a new certification at work might boost your career; or a wardrobe consultant to add some luster to your professional look; or maybe a public speaking coach to inject some bells and whistles into your business presentations. Personal growth often offers a faster and healthier return than financial investments. Hey, learning to play the guitar might be a lot of fun!

Personal growth is a powerful use of money. Books, lessons, seminars, and experiences all bring lasting value for the dollars spent. Some of that value might translate into increased earnings or lower expenses; some might add substance to life or lead to better use of precious resources. In almost every case, the value created exceeds the money spent.

I reject the notion that personal finance has to be boring. In fact, one reason many people fail is because they envision it as boring, and it very likely has been drudgery most of their lives. So the remedy to the boredom challenge is to add some spice in accomplishing goals.

No disrespect for the boring stuff, which has been well documented when it comes to personal finance. Every bookstore and library is crammed with "how to" financial books. Countless internet sites offer advice. Much of it is relevant and helpful, but knowing something isn't the same as doing it. That's where most people come up short.

For windfalls, blow it, mow it, and grow it. For all else, let's take a fresh look at some things you already should know. As humorist Will Rogers said, "It isn't what we know that gives us trouble, it's what we know that ain't so."

That's what we'll be looking at in subsequent chapters.

Chapter 2

The Shrinking Middle Class

> *"A strong, educated middle class is what made America the greatest country in the world."*
>
> — *Lincoln Chafee*

I've been managing money for over 30 years. I was a bank trust officer, then president of a registered investment advisory firm. I've worked with some great people and some very wealthy families, but I sure didn't start that way.

My parents were hardworking civil servants. Dad was a full-time Air National Guard sergeant and Mom was an elementary school teacher. My wife was a school counselor and we lived in modest, middle-class neighborhoods. Our children attended public schools and we share decidedly middle class values with most of our neighbors and friends.

America's shrinking middle class has drawn a lot of attention lately. It has become a topic of national discussion, especially in the political arena. Candidates from both parties decry economic and cultural issues related to a diminished middle class. That large group in the middle used to be larger, and it was much of America's economic strength.

In December 2015, Tami Luhby, writing for *CNN Money*, reported that the middle class has fallen from 62% of aggregate income in 1970 to 43% in 2015. Surprisingly, much of the migration was upward with some 49% of the population defined as upper class by the Pew Research Center[1]. Still, for the people left behind — and economic analysts throughout the world — income inequality is a huge challenge.

Some reasons for the shift are undoubtedly systemic. Increased automation and technology require advanced education. Global manufacturing has transferred some lower-skill jobs to other countries. An American shift from a manufacturing to a service economy hasn't been easy for certain workers.

But I suggest there's another reason. Many of the money practices held dear by middle class citizens are woefully outdated. Taught with the best of intentions, they were practical for a simpler era. Mom and Dad, to the extent that they taught us anything about money at all, imprinted our impressionable minds with some powerful lessons. But some of their cherished beliefs — good for their time — are powerfully wrong today. It's hard to "unlearn" lessons from our parents,

---

[1] Tami Luhby, "Middle Class No Longer Dominates In The U.S." *CNN Money* http://money.cnn.com/2015/12/09/news/economy/middle-class/ (December 9, 2015).

but remember our parents didn't have smart phones, GPS, or LASIK surgery, either.

In his book, *How Rich People Think*, author Steve Siebold, who has interviewed hundreds of rich people, explains, "It's not intelligence or education that holds back the average person from getting rich. It's the middle-class beliefs around money that keep them struggling to survive in a world of abundance." He adds, "The rich see money as a positive tool that has the power to create freedom and opportunity for themselves and their families.[2]"

Years ago, I came to the same conclusion. Some of our typical middle class money ideas and practices aren't very productive. In fact, some actually *hurt* our chances for financial success. The wealthy handle things differently, usually to their benefit. We can all learn some valuable financial lessons — and keep more of our money — by studying how wealthy people handle money.

The wealthy tend to avoid these middle class mistakes:

1: Price matters more than quality.

2: Neither a borrower nor a lender be.

3: Banks are the best place for investing.

4: Don't place all your eggs in one basket.

5: Extra effort always yields extra results.

---

[2] Steve Siebolt, *How Rich People Think* (London House, 2010).

6: The stock market is a casino.

7: Do-it-yourself and save money.

8: Advisors are for the wealthy.

Some people think they are doing the right things because they learned the wrong lessons, many of which came from family members or influential people who learned their wrong lessons from other family members or influential people. The lessons were believable because they come from believable sources. Maybe some were valid at one time, but that time is gone. Let's look for some new and better ways to think about money.

> *"To me bathtubs are the epitome of luxury. Either you have no money to own one or you have no time to use one."*
>
> *—Akilnathan Logeswaran, author*

Chapter 3

Price Matters More Than Quality

In his books, *The Millionaire Next Door*[3] and *The Millionaire Mind*[4], Drs. Tom Stanley and William Danko revealed that millionaires tend to make purchases with a practiced eye for the future. They buy top-quality merchandise based on the *lifetime* costs of ownership. Quality shoes or furniture may cost more up front but last longer and deliver better performance. The wealthy tend to purchase based on value instead of price.

A former banking colleague of mine repeatedly committed the same mistake. We were on the same purchase cycle with new automobiles. I'd choose a Honda or Jeep based on research and an eye towards resale value. Ignoring this methodical approach, he instead opted for the "cheapest" deal. Surprisingly, we often spent similar amounts.

But every three years when it came time to trade, I *always* got more money for my car — sometimes a lot more — and he

---

[3] Thomas J. Stanley and William D. Danko, William D., *The Millionaire Next Door.* (New York: Simon & Schuster, 1996).

[4] Thomas J. Stanley, *The Millionaire Mind* (Kansas City, MO: Andrews McMeel. 2001).

never understood why. He would blindly launch right back into his "buy the cheapest" cycle. An otherwise bright fellow, he was living proof that destructive buying habits are not confined to the uneducated.

An affluent client once explained to me how driving a Mercedes-Benz was no more expensive than driving a Chevy or Ford. He reasoned that operating costs and depreciation were less than with cheaper cars. I didn't do the math, but I do know that Mercedes-Benz autos have great resale value, which means lower annual depreciation. The up-front cost is markedly higher, but once you make the purchase, those numbers might make total sense.

Most consumer goods retain little liquidation value. If you owe a large balance on a big-ticket item — such as being "upside down" on an auto loan — it can be extremely difficult to unload without suffering a significant loss. The liquidation price for vehicles is called resale value. In real estate, it's called market price.

If you want to assess the value of an item, ask yourself what a sensible person would pay for it on eBay or Craigslist. That's the real measure of financial value.

Price is a dubious measure of lasting value. Many items — especially new consumer goods — reflect the costs of production rather than inherent value. The price of a new television or trendy headphones is based on manufacturing, transportation, advertising, and competition. The resulting price may or may not represent value.

Perhaps the best measure of value is a product's price as a used item. Stripped of the "commercial" costs, the item's true value is revealed. For products with inherent or collectible value, the used price might be close to the new price; for others, the new price is an expensive trap. Beware of falling into price traps, especially with borrowed money.

Chapter 4

Neither a Borrower Nor a Lender Be

Shakespeare said it first and Ben Franklin advised Americans similarly two centuries ago. It has since become a middle-class axiom. But their good intentions aside, there are different kinds of debt and not all debt is bad.

Borrowing on a credit card to buy consumer goods is almost always a bad idea. Borrowing to buy an affordable home in a good location is usually a good idea.

Many middle-class homeowners think it's a good idea to pay off their mortgage as quickly as possible, but knowledgeable wealth advisors typically discourage the practice.

Thomas J. Anderson wrote two bestsellers offering an opposing view: *The Value of Debt*[5] and *The Value of Debt in Retirement*[6]. He makes a strong case that properly managed borrowing can enhance a family's wealth. Businesses regularly borrow to make money and strategic borrowing can produce similarly powerful personal results.

---

[5] Thomas J. Anderson, *The Value of Debt* (Hoboken, NJ: Wiley. 2013).

[6] Thomas J. Anderson, *The Value of Debt in Retirement* (Hoboken, NJ: Wiley. 2015).

But the money for paying down a mortgage is no longer available for other, potentially more productive purposes. A mainstream economic principle called "opportunity cost" helps explain. In simplest terms, extra payments made toward a mortgage might instead be used for other activities, such as education or training to enhance earnings, starting a small business, acquiring rental property, or investing for retirement. Any of these alternatives might prove more profitable than paying off a low-rate mortgage, and if implemented properly, can be low-risk choices.

Consider a couple that decide to allocate an extra $500 a month toward paying down their 30-year mortgage. If that $500 were instead invested in a retirement account each month, assuming 8% annual growth, the homeowners would accumulate $734,000 at the end of the 30 years.

You might reason that putting $500 towards the monthly mortgage means it's paid off in half the time, and this means you could then start saving for retirement. Yes, you could, but to amass $734,000 at the same 8% annual growth rate, you'd have to sock away $2,100 each month for the remaining 15 years. You would no longer have a mortgage payment but not many people have those kinds of resources.

Borrow because it makes solid financial sense. Paying off a mortgage early negates *leverage*, one of real estate's top attributes (see Chapter 16). The advantageous combination of tax-favored interest and other people's money is hard to ignore.

Debt employed wisely magnifies wealth building potential. It's like using a lever to move a boulder: a little shove gets a lot of results. Conservative real estate borrowing can create immense wealth. But real estate tends to appreciate at a slow and steady rate, not unlike bank certificates. If you pay cash, your money is tied up in illiquid assets growing at a slow pace. Assuming you have cash, that money might be invested more productively.

Of course, debt opens a door that swings both ways. Great fortunes have been made with debt, but more than a few have been lost as well. It's important to use debt wisely. Always borrow conservatively; making sure you can comfortably meet the required payments.

Our wealthy friends understand the difference between good debt and bad debt. Perhaps a better adaptation of Ben Franklin's proverb is, "Neither a *bad* borrower nor a lender be."

Chapter 5

Banks Are For Managing Cash, Not Investing

Our parents loved banks, but our parents had far fewer options for their money. Mutual funds were not yet a credible alternative and money market funds didn't even exist 50 years ago. If the previous generation had a little extra money, they could buy a savings bond or put it in their passbook account. Banks offered money convenience, but little else.

Today, banks remain a fine place to manage cash but wealthy people rarely use them for investing. There are hundreds of alternatives and nearly all of them offer better long-term growth potential than bank deposits. The corner bank is where to maintain a checking account and emergency reserve, but your college account or retirement nest egg calls for a more productive approach.

A fellow visited St. Joseph last January for a job interview. When he got back home, he complained to his wife, "We could never live there. It's cold and blustery and there isn't a speck of green anywhere." A different visitor came home from a July conference. "Hot and humid," he explained, "why, I couldn't bear that heat without year-round air conditioning."

Both men had a brief experience with Missouri weather and drew opposite but equally mistaken conclusions. While each reaction contains a nugget of truth, neither conclusion was accurate. It all depends on when you visit!

A client once gave me the "bank rate" argument, saying, "I could have put my money in the bank and made as much as you made me through Family Investment Center." Another once commented, "A bank paying two percent a year would have made me more money." Like the Missouri weather example, while there may have been a nugget of truth to those two statements, their logic was dangerously flawed.

Earlier in my career, I spent fifteen years in banking. Banks attract money by offering a low rate that's assured versus the possibility of a higher one. Over the past decade, banks may have agreed to pay depositors a one or two percent annual return because they're certain they can invest the money elsewhere and earn more. That "spread" is what they retain as profit.

There's a reason why the biggest buildings in major cities are typically owned by banks. They know something that many consumers don't: guaranteed bank rates are typically 48 months or less, whereas most investments with greater growth potential have a longer horizon. In essence, banks pay customers a guaranteed low rate while using the deposits to reap more rewarding longer-term investments.

Bank accounts and certificates don't fluctuate in value because their principal and interest is guaranteed. Balances grow at a slow, predictable rate. Common stocks or longer-term government bonds change value on a daily basis because there's a vibrant market for them.

In order to attract investors, these longer-term investments must offer higher potential rewards. Higher quality portfolios containing stocks, bonds, or other investments inevitably endure some slower times, but financial products that fluctuate tend to reward long-term investors by compounding at a higher rate. Because of these fluctuations, there will occasionally be periods — usually short-term periods — when bank deposits outperform them.

Banks look better when other investments trend downward. Conversely, banks appear worse when equity markets soar upwards. Like our Missouri weather watchers though, neither of these circumstances is a true representation of long-term performance. With virtually any investment strategy, there will be intermittent times when having one's money in the bank would have been better. But bank customers trade performance for certainty and it's an expensive choice.

> *"Banks are run by executives, and executives protect themselves, and that does not always mean that banks are going to behave rationally."*
>
> — *Daniel Kahneman*

Middle-class consumers' affection for banks is often the result of remembering their parents' concerns about safety. Now parents themselves, they worry that other investments involve too much risk. But fear and worry are behaviors that lead to poor decision-making. In his book, *How Rich People Think*,[7] author Steve Siebold writes, "If the average person directed the amount of mental energy toward earning money as they do worrying about it, they would never have to worry again."

Worry and fear can lead to financial paralysis, the "deer in the headlights" syndrome that is so well documented in nature. (In fact, using bright lights to hunt is so predictably easy that it's illegal.) Sometimes, as with deer, things seem so frightening that people choose *not to do anything*. Immobilized by fear, they become statue-like spectators to their own financial destruction.

You have no doubt heard the adage that there will never be a better time to take positive action. It has been said so often perhaps people don't hear it anymore. Then too, rethinking your investment philosophy and restructuring your portfolio might involve acknowledging earlier mistakes. It might require changing how you research investment decisions. It may mean that it's time to dump the broker or other adviser responsible

---

[7] Siebolt, *How Rich People Think.*

for your disappointing results. These aren't easy decisions, but they are necessary considerations for future success.

Making changes may also provide a unique opportunity. Some of those earlier mistakes may translate into tax savings next April. Harvest some losses today and you'll feel better when tax time rolls around.

Chapter 6

Don't Place All Your Eggs in One Basket

I'm going to attack a sacred cow: something your parents or teachers probably taught you but something that is wrong. At the very least, your perception of what it means is mistaken. I hope you are open to new ideas.

Simple phrases teach important life lessons. Genius lies in packaging these lessons into memorable sound bites. Almost everyone can quote Ben Franklin proverbs and many of us carry dozens of familiar quotes — from a variety of sources — in our heads.

One such quote frequently repeated is, "Don't put all your eggs in one basket." It's become such a keystone investment concept that we created an impressive six-syllable word for it: *diversification*. Million dollar portfolios are constructed around the notion. Buying and holding a variety of investments is a good idea. In fact, it's a Nobel prizewinning idea. Professor Harry Markowitz received the 1990 prize for economics for his hypothesis and work developing Modern Portfolio Theory, the genesis of which was the concept of diversification[8].

---

[8] Harry Markowitz, "Portfolio Selection," *The Journal of Finance*, Vol. 7, No. 1 (March 1952).

What diversification *doesn't* mean is that it's better to have several stockbrokers or advisors. Why would two or three advisors be better than one? One will always outperform the others. Isn't this a recipe for dissatisfaction? Dividing your investments among advisors means no one has a "big picture" perspective of all your investments. Does it make sense to have accounts in several different banks? Only if you measure success by the amount of paperwork or driving miles. Does it not make sense to have everything financial in one place?

Today, you can achieve adequate or even superior diversification within one insured account. You can hold $1,000,000 of bank certificates — all insured by FDIC coverage — in a single account (and enjoy less paperwork and driving time). Adhering to the concept of separating your eggs, you can hire a dozen different investment managers within a single account. That account can hold both bank certificates and managed investment portfolios, and can be insured against institutional default up to *$100 million dollars*.

I'm talking mainstream personal finance here - stuff your parents and teachers would approve. Only, now, you have your different eggs in a completely different single basket.

Wealthy families commonly invest millions of dollars through one investment firm or bank trust company. Through thoughtful planning, they avoid the risk of brokerage or bank failure. They don't see this as dangerous, so why should anyone else?

There are practical benefits to working closely with a single advisor. It's easier to coordinate an investment strategy, ongoing filing and paperwork is greatly reduced, and the estate administration process is simplified upon the death of an account holder. Ask an experienced CPA about the burden of multiple statements and you'll begin to understand both the challenges and solutions.

Let that old proverb work for you. Shifting "all your eggs out of one basket" works even better when you can buy both eggs and baskets at bargain prices! The ideal time to create a superbly diversified portfolio is when the markets are down and the majority of investors have fearfully liquidated their stocks. It's the time to find bargains!

Whereas the best time to buy stocks is after a market plunge, the best time to hook up with a trusted advisor is now. Most of the marginal people have washed out of the investment business and the rest will soon join them. A sustained bull market like the 1990s attracts lots of friendly types. Tougher times require professional skill, experience, persistence, and a genuine desire to help clients. Competent advisors are survivors; your task is to find one.

Unlike the deer in the headlights, you have the ability to learn from mistakes. Most errors are correctable, but you must take action.

Chapter 7

Extra Effort Doesn't Always Yield Extra Results

I've served on dozens of charitable boards, even chairing a few. I'd routinely create agendas, monitor the time, and cancel unnecessary meetings. For me, a meeting is an avenue toward reaching a goal. Get together, have discussion, accomplish objective, adjourn.

Endless meetings drive me crazy.

It turns out that other people see meetings differently. For them, meetings are a social event. The point of meeting is, well, to meet. They get satisfaction from the activity, but not so much the accomplishment.

Many middle-class people derive similar satisfaction from investment chores. They spend hours on end studying stocks, bonds, mutual funds, and other investment options. They shop various banks looking for an extra quarter point return on a CD. They spend hours assembling annual tax information. It's all very satisfying activity...but not necessarily *productive* activity.

Spending a lot of time studying and shopping is no guarantee of generating better investment returns, especially for amateurs. Can researching a complex topic such as estate planning replace a knowledgeable financial professional? Does an extra quarter percent at the bank justify a tankful of gas or hours of your time?

The issue is productivity. As critical thinking exert Steve Siebold puts it, "Formal education teaches people how to think and perform in the linear world of commerce, but the rich rarely become wealthy trading time for money."[9]

How much do you actually earn for all that extra effort?

You don't perform every little personal or business chore yourself. Someone else mows the lawn or fixes the leaky faucet. You hire professionals to handle tasks beyond your proficiency. Accountants audit your books and prepare your taxes. You focus on your area of expertise and allow others to work in theirs. That's a pretty good approach to finance and investing, too.

More from Siebold: "The rich see themselves as team leaders, whether their teams consist of employees, partners, or outsourced contractors." In other words, they don't try to do everything themselves. They focus on their own areas of expertise and productivity.

Another reason the wealthy rely on advisors are the many variables inherent in personal finance. Retirement planning, for example, must take into consideration a person's age, income, health, spouse's health, genetics, children, geographic location,

---

[9] Steve Siebold, "New Report Connecting Intelligence to Wealth Is Nonsense," *Huffington Post* (June 22, 2013).

and lifestyle. Add in the level of investment sophistication and risk tolerance and you've created a complicated matrix for decision-making.

Another example is planning for educational expenses. How old are the children or grandchildren? How are their grades? What fields are they likely to study? Public or private college? In or out of state? Are there other sources of funding?

When you consider the complicated matrix for each of these goals, it becomes clear that no one should undertake these issues without professional assistance.

An area of planning that is frequently neglected is estate planning. Few people acquire a breadth of knowledge about wills through personal experience. For most, the will of a parent or older relative is their only encounter. To create their own will, they likely engage their family attorney.

Attorneys whose practices include any amount of estate planning have seen hundreds of wills, including ushering them through the complete probate process. They've witnessed family feuds, estate tax debacles, contested provisions and other legal entanglements. They have practical knowledge far beyond anything the average person has experienced. Their expertise is critical when dealing with legal documents.

Can you buy a "fill in the blanks" Last Will and Testament form on the internet or from the office supply store? Sure. Will it achieve what you want with the least amount of hassle and expense? That's a different story.

I recall a magazine article where the author bragged of having written his own will. He ranted against the high cost of lawyers (for clarification, I'm not an attorney) and professed that he'd saved hundreds of dollars. The whole process worked just fine, according to him.

What he didn't discuss in the article was that no one knows how well it works until after they are dead. For his family's sake, I hope he's right. I hope it flows effortlessly through the probate court and that no one contests the provisions. I hope they avoid estate tax surprises and that everyone is comforted by the results. And, for his family's sake, I hope they don't find out for a good long time.

Similar issues apply to investing. Even when someone is well informed about the markets, that knowledge is usually limited to a single situation or area. Typically, whatever acumen they may have acquired is based on one family's time frame with a single set of investment objectives. My encounters with people possessing some degree of financial savvy usually occur during market downturns. They visit our offices and recount their struggles. Invariably, they have enjoyed investment success during earlier investment cycles and have since learned — the hard way — that what worked during good times isn't much help during bad.

Capable advisors know when to request outside advice or service. There are numerous professionals in related fields from which to choose for help. *But that doesn't mean they provide equal talent, capability, or effort.* Good advisors know how to evaluate the strengths and weaknesses of other service providers and add value by acting as a filter mechanism for their clients.

One sign of expertise is a willingness to bring outsiders to the team when necessary, including local professionals such as attorneys, accountants, specialized insurance brokers, and others. Their recommendations may also include institutional custodians like Charles Schwab, TD Ameritrade, and Fidelity, or specialized investment managers, such as Dimensional or other fund families. They might also include real estate managers, art specialists, or antique dealers. As we've already discussed, there are hundreds of variables for each individual situation.

Enjoying or having a "passion" for something isn't the same as doing it well. As much as I love football, I don't imagine myself capable of playing professionally. My meager skills are better suited to sandlot football. The least talented member of the worst NFL team could flatten me in a nanosecond. My effort, however tenacious and determined, would fail to achieve success. Effort isn't productivity. Competence, experience, and the ability to work effectively with other capable professionals is more likely to translate into financial success.

Chapter 8

The Stock Market is Not a Casino

It's not unusual for middle-class people to believe investing means rolling the dice. Buying an individual stock is inherently risky, but buying a basket of diverse stocks can be *prudent.*

The basis of thoughtful wealth management is long-term diversification. It's a portfolio theory that has won several Nobel Prizes in economics. In essence, owning a wide variety of investments tends to enhance performance and reduce risk. There's a lot more to it, but that's the basic concept.

Many so-called "safer" options collapse under close evaluation. Comfort comes at a high price. Fixed income products such as bank deposits and government securities lose much of their gain to inflation and taxes. A bit of education about stocks and diversification can help put your mind at ease.

In his book, *How Rich People Think*[10], author Steve Siebold notes that education and attitude make all the difference: "When an economic correction occurs, the fear-based saver suffers catastrophic losses that may take years to recover. While world-class thinkers suffer similar losses, they quickly turn their

---

[10] Steve Siebolt, *How Rich People Think.*

attention to financial opportunities that present themselves in a society of suddenly terrified people."

Years ago, when I was a bank trust officer, I wrote an article explaining Modern Portfolio Theory (MPT) for the company newsletter. At a trust conference sometime later, a member of our firm submitted the article to a marketing pro for public review. The guy panned my article as being boring and uninteresting to consumers. That was an honest professional review, all right.

Between sessions, though, a fellow trust officer who was on our mailing list approached me and said, "I don't agree with that speaker. In fact, I thought your article was the best simple explanation of MPT I've ever read." Now that's a review to love!

What follows is a distillation of that article, minus some of the technical details. Whether you agree with the opinion of the consumer expert or the trust officer, I'll understand. Hopefully, it will provide you with a better understanding of MPT and help you thrive in today's investment world.

Up until the 1950s, most investment research focused on individual stocks and bonds. Which is the best stock for investors, Ford or General Motors? How do you decide between different corporate bonds? What methods of choosing predict the best purchase for a portfolio?

In 1952, the *Journal of Finance* published Harry Markowitz's pivotal paper, "Portfolio Selection.[11]" Over the next five decades, considerable academic research studied portfolio behavior.

In 1990, Markowitz, Merton Miller, and William Sharpe earned the Nobel Prize in economics for their long-term portfolio studies. That body of knowledge came to be known as Modern Portfolio Theory. It's tested and true, and stands as genuine investment science today. Like any science, the total body of knowledge continues to grow over time.

The key concepts relate to diversification. Not that investment diversification was a new idea, it wasn't, but some of the trio's findings rocked the investment world — and continue to rock it today.

First, it's important to remember that risk and reward are completely interrelated. That's the one absolute economic truth. It's always been understood that riskier investments tend to reward investors with higher returns, which is why, over the long haul, stocks tend to outperform bonds. Better performance is compensation for taking higher risks.

In investment research, portfolio fluctuation is used as the primary measure of risk. Dramatic portfolio fluctuations are more likely to produce a negative outcome.

---

[11] Harry Markowitz, "Portfolio Selection," *The Journal of Finance*, Vol. 7, No. 1 (March 1952).

What wasn't widely known before MPT is that mixing and matching investments can positively alter a portfolio's risk/reward profile. In fact, the most stunning finding was that mixing certain types of investments can *actually lower portfolio risk while increasing portfolio returns!*

Let that sink in for a minute.

Over years of professional investing, the common truth that runs from client to client and situation to situation is that everyone seeks high returns with low risk. It's human nature. Most of us are born with extreme risk aversion. New clients often remark, "I want something that pays high returns without any risk."

Now, after decades of academic testing, we discover (actually, they discovered; we just follow their work) that the right mix of investments can reduce portfolio fluctuations without hurting returns. At the very least, returns aren't reduced to the degree you might expect.

Think about two stacks of paper. One holds ten thousand dollars' worth of stocks, the other ten thousand dollars' worth of Treasury bonds. Most of us readily accept that the expected ten-year return from these stacks is quite different and somewhat predictable. Without quibbling over details, let's assume that the stock stack should grow at roughly ten percent annually, the bond stack at five percent, and let's assign a simple risk number to each: stocks with a risk of two and the bonds with a risk of one.

Now, if we mix the two stacks together to form a portfolio, we'd expect the annual return to be 7.5 percent, halfway between the two. Our expected risk should be 1.5, again, halfway between the two.

What Markowitz's research discovered, however, is that the returns are actually *above 7.5%* and risk *below 1.5*! Attributes of the stocks and bonds work together to increase portfolio returns while reducing risks. Clearly, the combined portfolio is better than the sum of its parts.

This was an absolutely revolutionary investment idea. And the "magic" works with virtually any mix of dissimilar assets. Mathematically, dissimilar assets are any investment classes with negative coefficients of correlation. Simply put, when one zigs, the other zags.

The upshot is that you can increase portfolio returns and reduce risks by matching real estate with stocks, or bonds or precious metals. The more diverse a portfolio, the more dramatic the improvement.

Though this improvement is counterintuitive, you can actually improve a conservative portfolio (raise expected returns and reduce fluctuations) *by adding some riskier holdings*!

According to MPT, a portfolio mix of eighty-five percent bonds and fifteen percent stocks should be safer and more productive than a portfolio of one hundred percent bonds! Believe me, before MPT, no one would have believed this! Some people still have trouble believing it.

There's at least one important disclaimer to this discussion. Though the science is very real, it's somewhat inexact. It's a bedrock concept for *long-term investing* but it doesn't have any predictive power. In fact, it argues against trying to predict the future. Rather, it suggests that a properly constructed portfolio will perform better with less risk over a wide variety of market cycles.

It's a bit like predicting the weather. The science is real and very helpful over time, but it is not accurate for every forecast all the time. MPT doesn't attempt to forecast the future; the science proves that diversified investors are rewarded with higher returns and lower risks across many market environments. There will be rough spots along the way, but takings risks and rewards into account, a Modern Portfolio will typically outperform others.

Chapter 9

Don't Self-Manage Your Portfolio

You've probably heard others say, "No one cares about my money as much as I do." Well, it's true: no one *does* care as much about your money. But caring about your money and effectively managing it are often two different things.

I've spent a career studying financial issues and helping people manage investments. I've passed licensing exams and met credentialing standards. I have graduate degrees in business and personal finance and I've started two successful investment companies. Chances are, I know more about managing money than you do because I have knowledge and professional insights you don't.

Caring about something doesn't always translate into positive results. It can be difficult to convince a loved one to make painful but necessary decisions. Consider how difficult it can be to use self-discipline when it comes to our health; it's even more problematic making tough financial decisions. Indeed, caring too much can be every bit as bad as caring too little.

Martin Luther King, Jr. told a story about an encounter between an old woman and young man in the midst of the

Civil Rights movement. The young man watched as she boarded a bus and made her way to the back row. “We don’t have to sit in the back anymore,” he explained gently. “Haven’t you been following the news? We’ve been protesting and marching for the freedom to sit anywhere we want.”

“I was marching right there beside you,” she countered. “Now that I can sit anywhere I want, I want to sit in the back where there’s more room for me and my packages.”

That story reminds me of the changes in the investment profession. Over recent decades, we’ve seen an amazing democratization. The emergence of mutual funds, discount brokerage firms, and unlimited access to technology has created a do-it-yourself investing revolution. Anyone with the time and inclination can do their own research and place their own trades.

Investment democracy is empowering. It grants investors the freedom to do something personally fulfilling. But just as rewarding is the personal freedom *not to do something*.

Technology brings new freedom to investors. Raw information and investment analysis is available to anyone on the internet and elsewhere. Trading costs have fallen while convenience and ease of use have risen. It's a terrific environment for do-it-yourselfers.

Some casual observers are even predicting the demise of investment professionals, although as you might expect, I’m skeptical. Without question, our industry is changing and I expect there will be a washout of less experienced or less knowledgeable advisors. As with any area of rapid change, traditional methods often implode as new methods arise. It's a natural progression. Thinning out the herd is a healthy development. Surviving advisors simply adopt new and better ways to serve their customers.

I once read an article noting that just fifteen percent of the investing population is truly "self-directed." That's an amazing statistic: *just fifteen percent!* I regard people who do their own investing as "hobbyists." They are highly enthusiastic, come from all walks of life, typically read *The Wall Street Journal* and personal finance magazines, subscribe to *Morningstar* or *Value Line*, and tune in non-stop to the financial news media. They follow the deficit, interest rates, and flows of capital across national borders. Their knowledge of detailed information often surprises me.

But I am speaking about a select few here. For the majority, personal finance is a casual pursuit. The immediacy of daily living takes precedence; financial management becomes a secondary concern. Most people, however well intentioned, simply don't have the time to follow the financial markets with the necessary dedication.

In fact, *most people don't want to do it themselves*, and among those who do, most do a poor job. The reason may be a lack of time, behavior biases, or lack of a plan, but whatever the cause for failure, I see it every day.

That's what the media misses. Most people are simply unwilling or unable to handle their own investments effectively. I have a suggestion for the journalists: stop writing for the tiny minority. Instead of writing (or talking) about fund performance, sector rotation, trade deficits, or (ridiculously) stock selection, spend some time helping people understand the complexities of the financial industry, its services, and fees. Provide some useful information about choosing and working with an advisor, and, if the situation calls for it, firing an advisor. Don't discuss these issues occasionally; talk about them every day!

One of the critical roles I fulfill for my clients is to serve as their *knowledgeable investment filter*. Investors are relentlessly battered by endless financial information from television, newspapers, magazines, internet ads, and even billboards. Some of it is news, some advertising, some a dangerous mix of both. Much of it is just loud and annoying noise.

In this climate, people need clarity: something to filter all the noise and find nuggets of genuine value. Most people are willing to pay for that help — eighty-five percent of investors, according to a popular magazine article.

Journalists hate secrets, and we've been hiding a huge one: a big chunk of people reading the newspaper or watching the nightly news are *already* working with an advisor. They are paying — in one form or another — for the financial help they want. If journalists truly want to help their audience, they should focus on solutions to the challenges investors actually face. Help them choose competent advisors with reasonable fees. Help them understand how to buy professional services. Help them find *value*. Become part of the filter, not part of the noise.

I find it instructive that prosperous people have quality advisors and less prosperous people don't. Do you suppose those folks have a lot of money *because* they have good advisors? You can manage your own money, but that's not what most wealthy people do.

Chapter 10

The Cost of Hiring Competence has Gone Down

Today's hyper-competitive environment and new disclosure rules are driving down investment costs across the board. That's great news for all investors, whether do-it-yourselfers or those seeking advice. In fact, it's never been easier or more economical to work with an investment professional, if that's your choice.

To help clarify this point about investment costs, I'll offer a brief review of business history. It's necessary to make a compelling point, but it will be quick, I promise.

The practice of commerce in America has followed three distinct stages. The first, born of the industrial revolution, was manufacturing. Companies took raw materials, molded them into products, and sold them to hungry consumers. There wasn't much variety, but it didn't seem to matter. Virtually a product-starved population devoured anything companies could make. Much of the country was agricultural and new gadgets eased a hard lifestyle. Henry Ford exemplified the early manufacturing phase. Asked about his Model T, Ford directed, "Give them any color they want — as long as it's black." Sales didn't suffer one bit.

Advertising ably represents the second phase. Manufacturing became more efficient and competition boiled over. Madison Avenue kicked into full gear and advertising bloomed with the advent of television. Now manufacturers made a product, but profits flowed through companies that *sold* it. Variety exploded as companies used differentiation as a sales technique. Cadillac fins kept getting bigger and fashion of all kinds became a principle of management. Give each salesman more to talk about and more sales will result.

Marketing is the third business phase and the one we inhabit today. The four Ps of marketing — product, placement, price, and promotion — have been around a long time. But consumer democracy (marketing's ultimate manifestation) is just beginning to settle in. And, like the famed Chrysler commercial used to say, "This changes everything."

Look at it this way. Products and services used to be distributed through rigid channels. You'd buy a new car from the dealership or telephones from the telephone company. You went to the record shop to buy music and a department store for clothes. Companies controlled product availability, information, and every step of the buying process. Perhaps we had a choice of stores, but we had to choose *some* store!

Where did consumers get genuine investment information? Where'd they go to buy an insurance policy? If they needed cash to buy something, where did they borrow? See, in the good old days of second-phase business, the consumer had little clout and even less information. *In this environment, sales commissions were a terrific management tool to sell everything from cars to mutual funds.* The customer could choose *which* stockbroker, but not *no* stockbroker.

It was a pretty good system except for one thing. *Commissions were never good for, never designed for, the customer.* Commissions were simply built into the price, and lacking another alternative, everyone paid them as a necessary toll for buying products. Since they were in every product, we silently bore the pain.

Way back in college, I learned that the perfect marketing company would "figure out what the consumer needed and offer it." I learned that the selling process would lose importance when knowledgeable consumers could easily seek out products and services. I learned that companies of all kinds would prosper when they truly integrated a customer perspective into their offerings. Two decades later, I still know these as truths.

In a world where quality information and terrific products are just a computer click away from almost everyone, second-phase companies no longer survive. Sales commissions are no longer a necessary toll and consumers won't pay them. That's not saying they won't pay anything. There are still legions of people who don't want to choose investments, and many of them seek advice and assistance. It's just that they'd prefer financial advice untainted by a sales pitch and commission.

Which brings us to today's investment industry environment. The investment world is extremely competitive. There's a stockbroker on every corner. There's a bank — with a discount broker in the lobby and a trust department upstairs — at almost every major intersection. Add in insurance agents and financial planners and it all begins to run together with alarming sameness.

But it's not really the same.

Many consumers focus on costs because it seems an easy (and important) thing to compare. If you are so inclined, you can visit a number of potential managers and collect their published fee schedule. You'd need to collect schedules from banks, brokers, investment advisors, financial planners, and (in some cases) insurance agents. By studying these documents, you'd probably arrive at a pyramid of costs.

This would be a great approach except for one thing: all options aren't equal. We aren't talking about a loaf of bread here, or two dealers offering identical cars. Instead, we are considering a field where there are thousands of products and widely varying degrees of professional competence. We're also working in the realm of horrendously complex cost structures amid an ocean of hidden fees.

Take that bank trust department, for instance. Costs shown on their schedule might omit profits they earn from their own family of mutual funds. It's also likely that very small print discloses other administrative costs earned from outside mutual funds. They probably get income from clients *plus* income from selected investment options. This isn't illegal or necessarily unethical, but it helps disguise the total costs you pay. Looking at the published fee schedule, it's unlikely that you would come away with a helpful understanding of total costs.

Similarly, just try to decipher the costs you'll pay in an insurance product or brokerage account. It seems so simple, but I guarantee that you'll go nuts trying to find a "bottom line" on these costs. Trying to compare costs within one industry is hard enough; across industries (insurance versus banking, for instance) is nearly impossible! It takes a carefully trained eye.

Equally important, all these options aren't equal anyway.

Does a broker equal an insurance agent equal a bank? Does quality of products or management matter? For that matter, are all stockbrokers equal? Does a new broker, fresh from a twelve-week training course, offer comparable value to the experienced professional in the corner office? Who offers better value: a fifteen-year insurance agent or a brand new trust officer? If you're getting ready to invest $100,000, who should you trust?

There's a fair chance that the bank's trust officer never passed a securities examination (trust departments are specifically exempted from the routine exams required of brokers, insurance professionals, and investment advisor representatives). In fact, the discount broker in the bank's lobby (where licenses are required) is potentially better tested than the trust investment officer!

None of this discussion is meant to slander competent professionals working in the investment arena. However, it does reveal some difficulty in evaluating investment services, especially on the sole basis of costs.

I created Family Investment Center after spending fifteen years in the trust/investment industry where I specialized in employee benefits and large IRAs, which offered unique insight into investment services and costs. I gained experience regarding industry fees and costs. Here are some important lessons I learned.

Commissions distort investment advice.

They tempt investment salespeople to recommend one option over others that might do a better job or cost less. In fact, the sales commission alone virtually assures that a product may cost more than other options in the marketplace.

I sometimes hear advisors say that they aren't personally influenced by sales commissions. Consider this: would brokerage firms, insurance companies, or banks (experts in generating income) use them as incentives if they didn't work? Of course not.

Similarly, "in-house" investments (banks or brokers offering their own mutual funds, for example) create a related distortion.

The need for profits compels the organization to favor these over other choices. Of course, there's also a built-in (and largely hidden) fee for consumers. Some groups offer a fee "discount" if you choose their products or funds, a discount often more illusion than reality.

Note also that in-house options often do not match performance offered through outside funds and managers. This may seem a small point, but it's not. If a firm recommends inferior mutual funds, then they are, in essence, placing organizational profit above clients' best interests.

Hidden costs are higher costs.

I once reviewed a company pension plan offered through a national trade group. My client insisted that it was free. Buried dozens of pages into the plan's prospectus, deep in the fine print, I found a disclosure of nine different charges taken against the account. *Nine different and expensive fees*!

In the investment business, sales skills are commonly more valued than investment skills. In a commissioned environment, survival requires sales skills. Products offered in this environment cater to consumer whims, not investment quality.

The crucial point is that it takes judgment, skill, and experience to properly engage investment knowledge for *your* benefit. Of thirty similar mutual funds, which one (or ones) is the best choice for your situation? Which one (or ones) melds with other securities to craft a quality, diversified portfolio? Which one (or ones) offers the best tax efficiency for someone in your circumstances?

All of that information is readily available for anyone willing to research it. You can dig it out yourself or you can hire someone to do it for you. The latter may be the better choice, given the low cost to hire someone today, because the old sales commission "toll" is gone. The price is much lower because the information is easily attainable.

Whether you do it yourself or hire it done for you, there is almost always a cheaper alternative (or something that *looks* cheaper), just like you can always find a cheaper lawyer or a lower-cost doctor. Truth is, every lawyer belongs to the bar association and every doctor holds a medical license, although it may be wise to remember that half the practicing physicians finished in the bottom half of their class. Chances are good, though, that you'll look beyond price in choosing the right person for your situation. Cost, while a factor, isn't the *only* factor.

Sales commissions still exist today and some investment firms using them continue to thrive. There are still modest markets for CD players and vinyl roofs, too. For reasons stated above and a few others, some commissioned products will always be with us.

The whole cost issue comes down to this: commissions were always good for the company and rarely (if ever) good for the client. I've heard the arguments and followed the trade commentaries. I've watched as some people turned this into a moral crusade. This is the practical truth as I see it: *the investment world has entered a Third Phase where the old methods can't last.* Old age, technology, and new regulations have inflicted a near-fatal wound to the investment commission system. It's never been easier or more economical to work with an investment professional.

Chapter 11

Many Mistakes Are Endorsed by the Media

At Family Investment Center, we make a concerted effort to garner media coverage. There's a practical reason for this: consumer distrust of the investment industry tends to devalue advertising. Many people simply don't *believe* investment advertising. Coverage by the media is more credible and so more desirable.

Several years back, I read about a local man who watched his family nest egg dwindle as the price of his employer's company stock tumbled. He had retired from the firm some fifteen years earlier, after working there for nearly four decades. A substantial portion of his net worth was tied to the fortunes of that one utility company. He was devastated.

Not mentioned in the story was the fact that any competent financial advisor would have recommended that he diversify his portfolio, as the risk of owning just one stock — any stock — is dangerously high. Those with disproportionately large holdings in a single company are at needless risk, even if the firm has a history of long-term stability.

The textbook solution to this problem is to implement a long-term plan where portions of the stock are liquidated in a tax-advantaged manner. But the local man likely never heard of the solution. Perhaps he was immobilized by worrisome media coverage, loyalty to his former employer, the desire to avoid taxes on his gains, or the prospect of paying for financial advice. Whatever the reason for his paralysis, he did exactly what he had always done when the stock price shuddered: nothing.

America is full of people like him: hardworking, honest folks lacking the information and tools they need to make solid financial decisions. The media bears some responsibility for this. Using a sort of Chamber of Commerce approach, they dance on eggs not to "favor" one investment firm or bank over another. This approach might be acceptable if every firm had similar knowledge and competence, but they don't. Training, education, experience, and professional judgment differ considerably from firm to firm and advisor to advisor.

When researching a story, the media frequently ignores the fact that some sources may not understand complex solutions or concepts. Never mind that they may have barely passed NASD licensing exams or that some licensed salespeople lack experience with solutions that do not involve the sale of a financial product.

Our friend needed *information*. He didn't need a stock tip, mutual fund, or municipal bond. He needed a practical solution to a very specific and complex problem.

Under the guise of being "consumer advocates," personal finance writers (who necessarily write for the masses) often support the antiquated notion that investors should "go it alone." While many people are capable of basic investment and finance decisions, suggesting that the average person tackle complex financial issues without professional help is like advising consumers to service their own cars. Given the proper training and experience, I suppose it's an option, but how many people have the knowledge, inclination, and time to perform such a complicated and potentially hazardous task?

There's an adage about people who "know the cost of everything and the value of nothing." I'm going to suggest that many of today's financial journalists fit this category.

Another time, I was being interviewed for one of those ubiquitous "financial makeover" columns. The writer and I listened to a very pleasant retiree describe her financial situation. After listening intently, I suggested that she could benefit from some ongoing professional advice and gently volunteered to propose some suitable advisors in her distant city. "She doesn't need that," the writer shot back, "I can help her pick some good mutual funds." The resulting column was well done but the writer's off-handed remark opened my eyes.

To save a few dollars on advisory fees, this writer recommends readers should go-it-alone. It's an attitude I see repeatedly in the media. And it's dead wrong.

Brokers emerged decades ago because people *needed* investment help. But as the profession expanded, it became increasingly sales-oriented, replete with onerous commissions and expenses. The do-it-yourself movement grew in quiet rebellion against those high expenses. The concept is an easy sell in a world of no-load mutual funds and readily available (usually free) financial information. Do-it-yourself is the antithesis of and a direct contradiction to the old way of doing things.

Well, wake up and sniff the Starbucks! Intense competition has created a brave new world where low or no-commission, quality help is available without sales hype. Dedicated professionals who deal with complex issues on a daily basis offer straightforward, unbiased information at reasonable cost. This is value-oriented advice that's affordable, understandable, and practical for today's investors and their families.

The majority of wealthy people I talk with simply don't want to do it themselves. For them, the relevant issue is how to find a competent advisor who offers value and understanding. They expect a relationship that is candid and beneficial for both parties.

Professional insight adds tangible value. Specialized knowledge about IRA withdrawal strategies might easily save ten of thousands in taxes or provide a similar amount in tax-deferred growth. Is a few hundred (or even a few thousand) dollars a fair price for that reserve of knowledge? How much needless anxiety and deprivation might that much money save decades down the road?

Tony Robbins does a great job in his new book, *MONEY Master the Game: 7 Simple Steps to Financial Freedom*[12]. In it, he outlines a variety of investment strategies and products. I think some are better than others, but it's a huge marketplace and there are many roads to investment success.

I think it wise to gain some investment knowledge, but ultimate success likely depends on having expertise in the narrower categories. In a way, Tony's book illustrates some of the real challenges of do-it-yourself investing.

Most investors do not understand that the investment world operates in layers. There is a retail/wholesale structure. The same investment product can be offered with several different pricing schemes. Often, smaller purchases impose higher costs, while larger buyers enjoy substantial discounts. Generally, personal service and smaller increments are signs of a retail operation. Storefront stockbrokers and insurance agents tend to be very retail, working with numerous smaller clients. Lower volume and higher personal service often mean higher prices.

Robbins talks about two products that prove this point. The first, *indexed annuities*, are widely known and marketed. There is a good chance you know someone who owns an indexed annuity. The appeal is that an insurance company investment

---

[12] Tony Robbins, *MONEY Master the Game: 7 Simple Steps to Financial Freedom* (New York: Simon & Schuster, 2014).

product guarantees stock market returns while protecting against losses. It's an "engineered" financial product that, on the surface, appears to offer the best of both worlds: higher returns, no losses.

But the devil is in the details. Indexed to what? There are dozens of investment indices and it really does matter which one the annuity is tied to. What is the participation rate? In other words, how much of the indexed return will the buyer accrue? Some annuities cap this return at 60-80% of the index's growth each year. Does that index growth include dividends? Some annuities do and some don't, but dividends can make a huge difference in long-term stock market performance.

Of course, there are all the normal annuity issues, too. How long must you invest? What is the penalty for early redemption? What is the insurance company's financial rating? A guarantee is only as good as the company offering it.

The challenge is that there are dozens of insurance companies offering indexed annuity products, but each one has different rules. As you can see, these rules can be complicated and confusing. In my experience, even the agents selling these products often don't understand them. This is especially true in the retail arena where local agents are calling on unsophisticated clients in their homes. Retail pricing is almost always the highest price for any product!

In summary, indexed annuities are a complex, engineered product offered by multiple independent suppliers, each with a captive sales force and related distribution fees. For the consumer, this potential for disaster abounds. Many people ultimately become disenchanted with their purchase.

Structured notes are another idea with a sound basis. They allow corporations or other groups to borrow money without a banker. Essentially, they package a loan as a security and sell it directly to investors. With no banker's profit, the borrower gets a better deal!

Think about how banks make loans. For each borrower, they insist on full disclosure of all relevant financial facts. Then they judge the economy, industry sector, management, competition, and other information. If they decide to make the loan, they make price adjustments (in the form of the interest rate) to compensate for extra risk. They may demand collateral in the form of assets or a claim on future earnings. They may require life insurance on key managers.

Structured note buyers face all of these same lending issues, but the consumer usually isn't in a good position to evaluate the risks or make pricing adjustments. There are also distribution fees (underwriting, administrative, and sales costs) deducted from the returns. Again, the more retail the product, the higher the fees.

Tony Robbins is clearly in a unique financial position — perhaps the top 1% of the top 1%. He most likely doesn't pay retail prices for any of the managers or products discussed in his book, making them much better products without high retail fees. But in addition to fees, there is also a legitimate issue about the expertise needed to evaluate and buy specialized products. Most consumers aren't sufficiently informed to make sound decisions about these products. Truthfully, I doubt that Tony understands all the issues, but he can afford knowledgeable experts to help him.

I love his book. I love that it includes honest information about the financial industry and its products. I love that he interviews the top minds in investing and shares their expertise and insights. I love that he is devoting his considerable talent to educating the public in an area where it needs quality education. My main concern is that readers might attempt some of these sophisticated and complex ideas on their own.

Books often need a "don't try this at home" warning!

Chapter 12

A Brave New World

In 2015, the President of the United States released a historic report titled, "The Effects of Conflicted Investment Advice on Retirement Savings."[13] According to the report, implementing a fiduciary rule could save families more than $40 billion over 10 years. A fiduciary must put the client's interest first in making investment recommendations or decisions.

This should be beneficial because the roles and expectations between advisor and investor will be more clearly defined, primarily due to the advisor's fiduciary responsibility. Removing the high-pressure sales environment should allow advisors and investors to interact with greater transparency, using client goals as the guiding focus.

This powerful idea encourages advisors to work exclusively for their clients' benefit. Advisors who believe a fee-only arrangement is a superior model will not accept sales commissions or other revenue, aside from a management fee. The fee-only format has become the trademark of a leading

---

[13] Executive Office of the President of the United States. *The Effects of Conflicted Investment Advice on Retirement Savings* (February 2015).

industry group, the *National Association of Personal Financial Advisors* (NAPFA), whose members agree not to accept sales commissions or non-client-based revenue.

There is some confusion regarding the difference between fee-only and fee-based arrangements. Fee-only refers to a fixed retainer or percentage of the overall amount in the portfolio. Fee-only advisors are already conducting business under the fiduciary rule, meaning their advice is always based on what is in the clients' best interests.

In contrast, fee-based advisors receive at least some of their income from commissions they earn selling investment products. Although some may work on a fee basis for certain clients, selling investment products (and earning sales commissions) may be a substantial part of their income.

Many middle-class people do not understand this important distinction. That's one reason for the President's report. Among other things, it explains:

- People who receive conflicted advice could see a 12% loss in potential growth in their IRA accounts over 30 years.
- Conflicted advice leads to far less productivity than taking advice from non-conflicted advisors

NAPFA and other professional groups understand that flexibility (in all things financial) is necessary to meet each individual's or family's unique needs. That's why fee-only (commission-free) advisors willingly compute payment for professional services in any of these ways:

- **Hourly**: Fees based on the actual professional and clerical time spent on your one-time analysis or service.
- **Project**: Maximum fees based on the estimated breadth and responsibility required for your one-time project.
- **Retainer**: A fixed or flat quarterly fee based on the estimated breadth, responsibility, and time involved in providing ongoing service to your accounts.
- **Investment management**: Fees based on the size of your accounts.

Fee-only advisors will *not* accept compensation from:

- Banks, brokerage firms, or mutual fund companies.
- Sales commissions.
- Transaction fees.
- Manufactured investment products (and levy fees for selling or using them in client accounts).

The opportunity for financial success may rise when investors receive unbiased, non-conflicted advice from investment professionals who cannot be swayed by commissions. These advisors are dedicated to seek out opportunities that best match the needs of the client.

Investors should consider which type of advisor best meets their needs. This is especially important as the fee-related vocabulary expands and gets increased media coverage, potentially causing even more confusion. Investors should come prepared with a list of questions, such as, what is the advisor's philosophy toward working with clients? How is the advisor compensated? How many economic cycles has the advisor experienced?

(See the Appendix for a more comprehensive list of questions.)

The Value Conundrum

Clients sometimes struggle balancing price and value. It can be a challenge to find "perfect" pricing for professional investment services.

Asset-based pricing — charging a flat fee, such as one percent annually — penalizes simpler accounts and undercharges more complex accounts.

Hourly pricing may not adequately reflect the value of the professional's expertise. What's a fair price for a recommendation that results in a meaningful gain in a client's ultimate wealth?

Retainer fees, while warranted by the extreme costs of research, technology, insurance, and staff, may seem even less acceptable to clients.

Project fees can be a good alternative. The obvious advantage for clients is being able to assess the value of a particular service against the price of obtaining it. However, clients may not recognize the longer-term value and the high cost of providing professional service isn't always apparent. In making value judgments, clients often underweight the potential value and overweight the price.

When choosing an advisor, investors should exercise due diligence. Ultimately, the decision is not as much about the money as it is about the people whose lives will be affected by the money: children, grandchildren, charities, and others the investor cherishes.

As the government and the media continue to highlight what "conflicted" advice truly means, here are some attributes to look for in an advisor:

> **Looks at the big picture**. This can help protect you from making emotionally driven responses during volatile market swings.

> **Maintains a client-centric approach.** Is motivated by your financial goals, not

commissions, and is willing to openly disclose how they are paid.

Good communicator. The advisor is easy to understand and doesn't try to impress you with verbiage or talk over your head. He or she takes the time to explain complex topics in understandable language.

Is appropriately licensed and credentialed. This might include a CERTIFIED FINANCIAL PLANNER™ (CFP®), Chartered Financial Consultant (CFC), Personal Financial Specialist (PSF), or other respected designation recognized by the financial industry. This doesn't mean an advisor must possess every certification. A long list of acronyms can't replace an advisor's genuine skill, experience, and dedication to investment success.

Fiduciary designation. The advisor has pledged to always act in your best interest, regardless of rules or guideline changes.

Chapter 13

An Aging Population Changes Retirement Planning

A form we use to collect retirement planning information from our clients includes a question about parents. A client asked me why. "Aren't most parents gone by the time someone retires?" he added.

Actually, thousands of retired people today have at least one living parent. In fact, according to the U.S. Census Bureau, more than 70,000 people in the United States have lived beyond the age of 100, and that number is expected to increase exponentially over the next 30 years. Ken Dychtwald, PhD, an expert on aging, reports that two-thirds of everyone in the history of the world who has lived to age 65 is alive today[14].

The growing number of elderly signals a vast change in America and retirement. Many who survived beyond age 100 have outlived their money and depend on Social Security, public assistance, and their families to make ends meet. More and more people now enter retirement with a living parent.

You probably learned about retirement from your parents or grandparents, but their knowledge has little relevance to today's

[14] Ken Dychtwald and Daniel J. Kadlec, *The Power Years* (Hoboken, NJ: John Wiley & Sons, Inc., 2005): 13.

world. According to a National Institute on Aging (NIA) study, in 1960 the typical retiree worked for 46 years and lived one year after retirement. By 1995, the average retiree worked only 37 years and lived another 12. Today, the average worker lives 18 years after retirement!

It's difficult to overstate the impact of the aging population. The Dychtwald book notes that, for the first time, there are more adults over 65 than children under five[15]. That means the next social revolution could be about aging issues. French workers rioted when their government wanted to raise the national retirement age.

Why does this matter to you? Changing demographics will affect your financial behavior in four areas:

- **Income.** Retirees in the U. S. today report that 39% of their annual income comes from Social Security. Lifelong pensions are a relic of the past, so where will you get the income you need?
- **Retirement plan distributions.** Most corporate pensions have been replaced by 401(k) plans. Responsibility for a secure retirement has been transferred from corporate America to its employees. How will you invest a lump-sum retirement

[15] Ken Dychtwald and Joe Flower, *AGE WAVE How the Most Important Trend of Our Time Will Change Your Future* (New York: Bantam Books, 1990): 8.

distribution? Can you balance risk and reward? Can you generate income and still preserve buying power over three decades of retirement?

- **Investments.** Stocks? Bonds? Annuities? Mutual funds? Will you use an advisor or an online brokerage? These become critical issues when you need to preserve assets while generating income over an extended retirement.
- **Estate planning:** The estate-planning conundrum grows exponentially with the size of your family. Contrast the degree of planning necessary when people only lived a year after retirement with today, where five-generation families are not unusual.

A big mistake retirees make is ignoring the need for financial flexibility. Meeting today's retirement needs requires the ability to adjust your plan as the future demands change. That requires a sufficient time span.

How much were you earning back in 1980? What kind of house did you live in? What did your family look like? Fast forward to 2040. How much money will you need? Where will you live? How many descendants will you have? That's only 24 years in the future; many of you reading this will still be alive then.

These are critical retirement issues and the reason why we ask about parents when we collect retirement-planning information.

Chapter 14

It's Not About the Money

Since beginning my career as a bank trust officer in 1984, I've had thousands of conversations about money. I've listened carefully as clients and friends discussed new homes, autos, vacations, businesses, and schools. I've enjoyed helping my clients save and spend millions of dollars. I've reviewed countless financial statements, balance sheets, and investment recommendations. I've studied columns of numbers until my eyes blurred, blinked a few times, and then studied them some more.

After 30 years of listening, here's my conclusion: great financial planning is not about the money. It took me a while to learn that. Education and training in financial services is not what provides value to clients; it's the incremental tidbits of knowledge that an advisor accumulates over decades.

I've been fortunate to learn my craft at the feet of some financial masters, among them a crusty New Yorker named Nick Murray whose columns and books I fervently recommend. I constantly marvel at Nick's wisdom and offer the following insight as an example.

Murray identifies Five Great Goals of Life[16]. To paraphrase, they are: comfort in retirement, financial assistance for children, educational assistance for grandchildren, care for aging parents, and gifts to charitable organizations. Not everyone aspires to all five, but most people can identify with something on the list.

There's nothing overly surprising about these goals. It's a well thought-out list (Nick is a smart fellow and doesn't miss much), but fulfilling all of these goals can be intimidating. While we all hope for a fulfilling retirement, people are often oblivious to the personal commitment needed to meet the other "great goals."

Did you notice that none of the five are "money" goals? The focus isn't on building wealth; it's on *taking care of people and institutions we love* — our spouse, children, parents, and church. These are *people* goals! In today's world, that's remarkable insight.

Our ability to meet these goals is enhanced by accumulating *value*. The terms *money* or *investment* are too restrictive. Building equity in a home creates financial value, but it isn't money or an investment. Most parents positively influence their children's lives on a daily basis, yet think of the even greater impact they might have by providing more value: a quality education, travel and cultural experiences, business

[16] Nick Murray, *The Excellent Investment Advisor*, (Nick Murray, Publisher. 1996).

opportunities, and the freedom to pursue special talents or abilities.

Although the five goals are about people rather than money, our financial success largely determines our ability to achieve life's important objectives. *The better we do financially, the more powerful our positive touch in the lives of people we love.*

Your best chance for accumulating financial value is to work backwards from each goal. None of these goals are unattainable if you implement systems to save, invest, and monitor financial value. These can be really simple systems involving rational investment choices, disciplined spending, automatic investment plans, and periodic financial checkups. These are the tools that can make the dreams of the people in your life a sweet reality.

Building financial value needn't be a complex process, but rather a systematic approach of analyzing options and choosing those with the best chance of accomplishing your goals. It really can be that simple. You merely need to make modest sacrifices for the people you love.

After all, *money is just a tool to help us meet the Five Great Goals of Life.*

Chapter 15

Women Have Unique Financial Needs

Women control much of the world's wealth. One reason is that they tend to outlive men. The wealthy widows of the world own a lot of financial assets. In fact, most women will be alone — and in charge of their assets — at some point in their lives.

The 14th Annual Transamerica Retirement Survey of Workers[17] contains some revealing responses by women:

- Only 7 percent are very confident in their ability to retire comfortably;
- Roughly two-thirds of Baby Boomer women have no backup plan should they be forced to take early retirement;
- 43 percent of women do not have plans to retire or expect to work over the age of 70;
- 45 percent of women work part-time jobs and thus are less likely to be given retirement benefits.

---

[17] Catherine Collinson, Fourteen Facts About Women's Retirement Outlook (Transamerica Center for Retirement Studies, 2014) www.transamericacenter.org.

While alarming, these responses reveal the unique needs and opportunities women have when it comes to investing, which is different for women than for men. One reason is their longer lifespan. While, on average, women may work fewer years than men, they typically live about six years longer, which means they need more money for retirement[18]. Social Security benefits can help women ease the shortfall, especially if they wait to start drawing down benefits until later in life (something a financial advisor can explain in more detail).

It's especially important for women to have sound investments in their portfolio but uneasiness or lack of confidence about investing can be a barrier. In fact, Forbes reported on something called the *female financial paradox* in a 2014 article titled, "Closing the Confidence Gap: Women and Investing."[19] It describes how women are "a growing economic force, expected to add $6 trillion in earned income globally over the next five years ... yet many women lag behind men when it comes to using those assets to plan and build financial security for the future."

In my experience, many women — particularly divorcees and widows — keep their money in low-interest accounts because they lack a reliable investment strategy or are so averse

[18] U.S. Department of Labor, Employee Benefits Security Administration, "Women and Retirement Savings."

[19] "Closing the Confidence Gap: Women And Investing," *Forbes magazine*. (May 7, 2014).

to risk that they choose not to take any risks at all. If the husband made the investment decisions when they were married, the wife may lack the confidence to choose investments. Women may also be more likely than men to preserve their wealth, and so forego opportunities for higher investment returns.

Although they are as likely as men to enroll in company retirement plans, women tend to contribute less. It's an area where they could do better by fully participating, taking advantage of the company match, and making it a point to never invest less than the company is willing to match.

Another difference is how the two sexes perceive the responsibility for making investment decisions. In the *Forbes* article, a financial advisor at Northwestern Mutual noted that women have more power and earning potential than they've ever had, but many are placing others in the position as head of the household and relegating investment decisions to that person, often the husband. Taking a more team-based approach on the discussions regarding investments could open more doors in the future.

Here are some planning tips for women, based on my experience.

Put yourself first. This may sound selfish, but women tend to be perpetual caregivers, often to the detriment of their own finances. It's honorable to give to charitable organizations or pay for your child's college tuition, but be sure your financial plan can accommodate that goodwill. If you sacrifice your retirement savings to help your children today, who will take care of you when your savings eventually run dry? (Like the airplane oxygen mask, you have to put on your own mask first to be able to help those around you.) You must also get past any guilty feelings. When it comes to investing for retirement, accommodating what you think others want you to do may not serve your best interests — or theirs — later.

Be involved. Participate in employer-sponsored retirement plans and, if you can, be sure to contribute at least as much as your employer matches. If you can, sock away additional savings in an IRA as well. Keep tabs on the components in your financial plan. Know what you have, where it's held, how it's invested, and how to access it. I've seen women become widows unexpectedly and because their late husbands managed the finances, wives were left not knowing how much they had or where the assets were held. Some didn't even have passwords to gain access to the information.

Educate yourself. Don't rely on the advice of friends — however well intentioned — for investment advice. Most don't know any more than you and even if they do, what's good for them may not be good for you. You may not feel comfortable about investing, but smart investing is crucial to meeting long-term goals. I find that people who don't know much about investing are sometimes embarrassed to admit it. In some instances, they've been frightened by horror stories from others, many of who might have been do-it-yourself investors. The markets can appear intimidating to someone who doesn't understand diversification or how long-term market returns work. Some join investment clubs, which can be a great tool for gleaning investment knowledge, but never hesitate to consult with an experienced financial professional for expert advice. Also know what resources will be available to you when you retire. Familiarize yourself with Social Security and Medicare so you don't miss out on your promised benefits.

Find an advisor with whom you feel comfortable. Some financial professionals are stodgy, bureaucratic, and generally unwelcoming.

Find an advisor you feel comfortable asking questions; find someone who instills trust, has a clean history, and has proper credentials. Websites like www.SEC.gov and FINRA's BrokerCheck allow you to research disciplinary histories. Sites like www.NAPFA.org help you find advisors who will put your best interests first.

Learn about the many Social Security strategies. Men and women are wired very differently! For example, many women, even professional women, let their spouse handle the investment and retirement planning. Don't make the mistake of being uninformed about those decisions. Get involved. Learn about how to elect drawing your Social Security benefits. Men seem to be more inclined to begin benefits as soon as they retire. This can be a financial mistake costing hundreds of thousands of dollars. Couples need to understand the various strategies for drawing benefits in order to maximize their lifetime benefit. A critical consideration is how much the surviving spouse — most often the woman — will be left with as her lifetime benefit. There are a host of strategies for claiming your Social Security benefit. Make sure you understand them before making your election. Whether married, single, divorced, or widowed, you need to know your options.

Imagine what your retirement will look like. How do you wish to spend your retirement? Sometimes, the things we enjoy doing occasionally lose their allure when we do them all the time. A client who loved the ocean retired and bought a beachfront cottage. After a year, she moved back home and went back to work. She discovered she could only walk on the beach so much!

Think twice about insurance. Retiring before age 65 could be costly once you lose your employer insurance benefits. Make sure you factor in all retirement expenses.

As to the aforementioned penchant women have for spending too much on others and too little toward retirement, working with an investment advisor can help provide a confidence boost as you move toward your long-term goals without sacrificing the moments you want to experience today. Your female intuition can also contribute to helping you succeed because at every step, you'll be able to identify the emotions and attitudes that impact your financial decisions.

Chapter 16

Pay Off Your Mortgage and Ruin Your Retirement

Some advisors still recommend paying off mortgages early, especially before retirement, but many are reconsidering that notion. It may be the result of continued low interest rates or a changing middle class attitude about debt. Like any financial advice, the right answer depends on your circumstances. Whatever your belief, there's an alternative approach that merits attention.

Financial decisions can be complicated and sometimes the value may seem less obvious. The objectives they are based on aren't always clear, whether buying a car or buying an estate. Decisions affecting your retirement can be particularly challenging. According to Bankrate's Financial Security Index, 36 percent of Americans aren't saving for retirement. Advisors are working to change this oversight by helping clients think about their financial health in new ways.

One strategy that is being reevaluated is the conventional wisdom of paying off the mortgage early to escape debt. According to the 2015 Federal Reserve Board *Report on the*

Economic Well-Being of U.S. Households[20], 67 percent of homeowners have a mortgage. The average monthly payment was $1,225 with the median at $1,100. Another report from Pew Charitable Trusts declares the median home loan balance is $103,000.

That data may seem alarming, but is retiring while still in the grips of debt really that bad? No, and here is why. Intentional debt can help build wealth. Just as businesses use financial leverage successfully, individuals can use their mortgages to work for their financial futures.

An economic principle called opportunity cost helps explain. In simplest terms, extra payments made toward a mortgage might instead be used for other purposes, such as starting a small business, acquiring rental property, saving or investing for your retirement. Any of those options might prove more profitable than paying off a low-rate mortgage. And, if done correctly, they can be low-risk decisions.

Consider a homeowner who decides to pay an extra $500 a month toward the mortgage. If that amount was invested in a retirement account for the typical 30-year life of the mortgage and assuming 8% annual growth, the homeowner could have amassed $734,000 during the same time period.

Yes, putting $500 monthly towards the mortgage could pay it off in half the time, after which that amount could be

---

[20] Federal Reserve Board *Report on the 2015 Economic Well-Being of U.S. Households (May 2016).*

invested for retirement. But assuming the same 8% annual growth rate, to get to that same $734,000 mark the homeowner would have to sock away $2,100 a month for the next 15 years. He would no longer have a monthly mortgage payment, but he would have to more than *quadruple* his monthly savings contribution!

Mortgages Can Also Be Wealth-Builders

> Turmoil creates both peril and opportunity. Falling property prices may offer the opportunity for a bargain, but only if you can afford to wait out the chaos before selling again. Your opportunity may be at the expense of a distressed individual or developer but you don't want to become the next distressed seller! Investors in real estate enjoy leveraging opportunities not found in most other investments. Executed properly, the strategy involves methodically paying down mortgage debt as the property rises in value. Borrowing costs tend to be low because the collateral is considered rock solid.

Certain Trends Suggest Rare Buying Opportunities

A badly distressed real estate market is a buyer's market. People who for various reasons shouldn't have bought earlier are struggling with their mortgages and foreclosures are way up. Prices on everything — homes, condos, apartments, even commercial buildings — are way down. Housing prices are driven by many factors; substitution is a powerful one. That's why appraisers use "comparables" (comps) to estimate value. Even new properties are affected by the falling price of existing homes. Simply put, all prices fall in a slump.

Vacation and second homes aren't immune either but they have a feature that makes them particularly desirable. Buyers don't necessarily have to sell one property to buy another, the way most homeowners do. Lower prices on something you want to buy aren't much help if you need to sell your existing property in the same troubled market. For this reason, buyers of vacation or second homes almost always have an advantage in the real estate market.

Demographics Are Another Powerful Factor

Typically, people in their fifties and sixties have extra money. Their peak earning years coincide with reduced family expenses to generate remarkable cash flow. Baby boomers will ride this wave of cash for the next decade or so.

What should they do with this excess cash? Well, investing for retirement is a logical choice and many will follow that path. But traditional investing may not have the allure to attract every retirement dollar. A lot of people may consider real estate as an option. Vacation homes, especially, meld two intriguing ideas: investment potential and family fun. It's an appealing package for aging baby boomers and other affluent investors.

From a financial perspective, purchase price, interest rates, and rental income are the main decision variables. Potential appreciation is the biggest mystery as it's always tough to peg. The cost of new construction rises over time and that impacts the substitution factor. Location is critical, as is demand. Housing styles go in and out of favor, and so do regions and neighborhoods. But despite these variables, one thing seems likely: Property will be worth more tomorrow than today. The longer you own it, the more likely that is to be true.

Don't Use Cash To Buy Real Estate

There are several reasons for this, the most persuasive being that it negates one of real estate's biggest advantages: leverage. The combination of tax-favored interest and Other People's Money (OPM) is hard to ignore. Borrow only when it makes solid financial sense.

Real estate tends to appreciate at a slow and steady rate, comparable perhaps to bank certificates. Pay cash for real estate and you tie up much of your wealth in illiquid assets growing at a slow pace. And, assuming that you have cash in the first place, that money might be invested more productively. Why deplete productive investments?

Of course, debt opens a door that swings both ways. Great fortunes have been made with debt, but more have been lost. It's vital to use debt wisely. Always borrow carefully and make sure you will have sufficient income to meet required payments.

Vacation And Rental Properties Offer Potential Income

Strangers will pay to stay in your property. Rental properties generate monthly income; vacation properties can provide weekly or daily income. Either way, outside income helps pay the mortgage and upkeep. Renters help pay for the property.

History provides countless examples. Villas on a popular lake or cabins overlooking a scenic canyon in the mountains are almost guaranteed to grow in value. Find a ten-year-old newspaper and check out the real estate ads. You'll be amazed (and possibly sickened) to discover what you might have bought a decade ago, and how that "astronomical" price at the time has shrunk in comparison to today's prices.

Key Lessons in Real Estate

A depressed market creates enormous opportunity for first-time homebuyers and buyers of second and vacation homes.

Keep yourself in position to buy without having to sell something else first.

Maintain good credit and have adequate income available for buying opportunities.

Choose property with both income and appreciation potential.

Buy property you like well enough to keep through real estate slumps.

Take a moment to consider what might be holding you back from putting more money towards your retirement. A 2013 Employee Benefit Research Institute survey found that 30 percent of respondents said job uncertainty and making ends meet keep them from investing toward their retirement. Just over 40 percent said their day-to-day costs keep them from considering a retirement strategy. Others may harbor habits, emotions, and attitudes toward money that prevent them from taking the next steps toward building their retirement.

In many ways, that template represents normal and expected behavior. But many times, the foundation of the struggle is a well-worn path toward conventional wisdom, and conventional wisdom is a lot like fishing off your own dock; easy and fun, but rarely rewarding.

My suggestion? Hire a qualified guide and seek out the sweet spots. No guarantees, but my guess is that you'll be happier and more successful.

Chapter 17

Money Disorders Sabotage Great Intentions

There is strong anecdotal evidence that financial success is linked more to behavior than income. We see this all the time in our office: people with high income and low net worth, or, alternatively, people with low income and high net worth. What accounts for these differences? Is it the money or is it the mind?

Drs. Ted and Brad Klontz, father and son psychologists, recently authored a book called *Mind Over Money*[21], published by Broadway Books in New York. It's a breakthrough of sorts, perfect for readers in the medical or other professions. It features both clinical and personal insights, as well as considerable research and a detailed bibliography.

The book's premise is simple: financial issues are clouded by psychology. Money evokes emotions such as stress, fantasy, irrationality, and fear, among others. Powerful feelings, all, that can distort the best possible financial intentions. Why is it, they ask, that we *know* the right things but *do* the wrong things?

---

[21] Brad Klontz and Ted Klontz, *Mind over Money: Overcoming the Money Disorders That Threaten Our Financial Health* (New York: Broadway Books, 2009).

The authors identify twelve disorders and recount both observations and explanations. To add some gravity to this discussion, the Drs. Klontz note that American Psychological Association surveys show that Americans rate money as life's number one stressor — higher than work, health, or children. Some research suggests that money disorders may be more prevalent than anxiety or depression.

I'll not list all the disorders here, but most will be familiar to physicians: hoarding, dependency, enabling, denial, and rejection. The spending disorders are witnessed frequently and fall into three broad categories: Money-Worshipping, Money-Avoidance, and Relational disorders.

Everyone exhibits some of these behaviors at one time or another. Everyone occasionally helps family members or keeps a collection of silver spoons in the kitchen. Those don't rise to the level of genuine disorder until they sabotage family finances. The symptoms are easy to spot: constant financial anxiety or despair; lack of family savings or excessive debt; multiple bankruptcies or defaults on loans; financial conflicts with family or friends. Again, it's not an occasional bout with these issues, but long-term, recurring, and unresolved problems that signal a disorder.

- Hoarding: A Money-Worshipping Disorder. Where is the line between hobby and obsession? When the new Lamborghini or another exotic vacation robs resources from the kids' college account, it's a legitimate problem.
- Enabling or Dependency: Relational Money Disorders. How many times must we toss a financial lifeline to adult siblings or children? It takes at least two people to play this game, and it's financially destructive for both.
- Denial: A Money-Avoidance Disorder. "I don't deserve to have money. Financial issues like retirement and education will take care of themselves. I don't deserve money. Money is bad. Success might ruin me."
- Rejection: Another Money-Avoidance Disorder. "My uncle was evil, and I don't want anything to do with his money. All rich people are greedy. I need to spend lottery winnings quickly. Inherited money is poison."

The daunting challenge with any disorder is a pattern of continuing behavior. Without intervention, either personal or clinical, destructive patterns rarely stop on their own. It's that repeating cycle that wreaks havoc.

Thankfully, there are exercises and techniques to address these problems. While flagrant cases might require clinical intervention, enlightened self-treatment can be effective in most instances. A growing number of financial and mental health professionals train or research in this field. The Financial Therapy Association (www.financialtherapyassociation.org) and the *Financial Therapy Journal*, for example, offer cutting edge research and knowledge.

The gist of this message is that money really matters. Financial health is critical to both patients and our own families. People need money for daily expenses but they also need money for a healthy life and retirement. Financial health is an important component of overall wellness.

Good Tax Planning Requires Forethought

A routine challenge for financial advisors is the frantic client clutching a recent tax return. "Oh, my God," they moan, "I just came from my accountant's office and I owe $10,000. I don't have the money."

Sometimes it can't be helped. The client had a large bonus come around or sold a piece of property for a large gain. Sometimes, they earned a one-time consulting fee or landed a publishing contract for the novel they've been writing. Taxable events, all, but the income taxes arise from a sizable cash payment, and who really complains about that?

Most of us won't see a payment like that this year and we still face occasional tax surprises. Those surprises are maddening, but there are a few tricks to keep them tolerable.

First, it's important to remember that most personal tax is computed using a calendar year. So, April's surprise is already ancient tax history. There is little to be done after the fact. Good strategy is done in real time, with a bit of research, recordkeeping, and deliberate decision-making. Most taxes are saved by not incurring them in the first place.

Let's consider a few scenarios. Suppose you encountered an opportunity to buy a commercial property at a discounted price. IRS Section 1031 offers a way to "roll" the proceeds of one property into another similar property without incurring capital gains taxes. It requires an escrow account, suitable replacement property, and both transactions must occur within a specified time period. Most title companies can handle the paperwork.

Section 1031 exchanges take place all the time, but they only work with careful planning. Since capital gains can be sizable, advance planning could postpone a huge tax liability. Eventually, of course, property will be sold and taxes paid, but why pay before you have to? Why pay this year?

Retirement plans provide another good example. They come in a variety of shapes and sizes and some are suited to sole proprietors, while others to partnerships or corporation. They can be cheap or expensive, small or large, and simple or complex. Most require some setup and adoption before tax year-end. Again, a bit of forethought allows you to direct dollars to retirement instead of Uncle Sam.

The same principle holds true for charitable giving. Generally, gifts given by December 31 count toward that year's tax. Since taxes typically aren't prepared until April (much of the required paperwork doesn't come until late January or after), it's hard to measure tax impact without some late-in-the-year projections. My suggestion? Sit down with your accountant each December to "mock up" that year's income tax so you can reach informed decisions about giving.

Remember the three steps cited earlier: research, recordkeeping, and deliberate decision-making. Solid information is a few clicks away on the internet or readily available at the library or bookstore. Study back issues of *Kiplinger*, *Barron's*, or other professional journals. If you don't want to do the research yourself, hire an advisor or ask your accountant.

Don't wait until your taxes are prepared or due before acting. The time to save on this year's tax payment is last year. The time to save on next year's tax payment is now.

Chapter 18

Small Businesses Create Wealth And Planning Issues

Small businesses are a powerful economic force. The Small Business Administration (SBA) says ninety-nine percent of America's businesses are small, yet they provide the overwhelming majority of new jobs[22]. Truly, today's entrepreneur is the hero of our economic system.

When it comes to retirement, however, these American heroes face daunting financial obstacles. The SBA also explains that fewer than half of all new businesses survive for five years. Every month, thousands of small businesses close their doors. When this happens, community jobs vanish along with the owner's dream. Employees are left to fend for themselves.

Noted financial advisor Nick Murray describes "comfort in retirement" as a universal financial goal[23], something *everyone* wants. Small business owners wrestle with some special challenges in getting there. Small business employees face peril if those challenges can't be met.

Financial Issues

---

[22] "Facts About Small Business in America." *Business Insider* (2011). www.businessinsider.com/facts-about-small-business-in-america-2011

[23] Murray, *The Excellent Investment Advisor*.

One problem is the failure to plan. It can take years to prep a company for sale. Certain aspects of business finances might be adjusted to be more appealing to buyers; family members might be removed from the payroll; owner benefits could be eliminated. Prospective buyers want to know if the company will continue to be profitable after the original owner retires. Are systems in place to duplicate the owner's skill and dedication? Will key employees stay on and continue to care for customers?

Some of these issues can be addressed through a formal succession plan. As an owner approaches retirement age, subtle shifts in operation can help answer important buyer questions. Key employees or family members might be groomed for future leadership. Perhaps accounting changes or internal investment programs can be implemented to fund a future buyout. A little preparation goes a long way.

Capital gains taxes play a huge role in this plan. Many small businesses start on a shoestring but are worth much more by retirement. The gain in value is taxable to the original owner. Careful planning can help postpone or avoid taxes, which can amount to thousands or even millions of dollars. Although capital gains taxes are currently at a lower rate than regular income tax, a 20 percent chunk of a million-dollar gain is a big check gone to Uncle Sam.

There are techniques to minimize taxes due upon sale and they are worth exploring. Accountants and attorneys may suggest an installment sale, stock swap, or other ideas to reduce taxes. Each strategy has advantages and disadvantages, including the pluses or minuses of a cash sale. The ramifications should be carefully considered. Of course, buyers want to minimize taxes, too, so the process can become pretty complex.

Who are the likely buyers for a business? Generally, it's someone within the family, key employees, or a competing firm. Most entrepreneurs would like to see a family member step in, but that's not always possible. Not every family has a likely successor and money to purchase may not be available. How can an owner get fair value and retire if a worthy but underfunded family member wants to buy the business?

Some experts suggest that only a small portion of family businesses pass to a second generation, and even fewer make it to a third. A family transition may be the founder's dream but it's not often realized.

Selling to employees or competitors is more likely. Some firms create an Employee Stock Ownership Plan (ESOP) as an avenue to shift ownership. This approach offers some attractive tax benefits but it's a complicated process that may require several years (and thousands of dollars) to accomplish objectives. Still, in the right circumstance, it can be a practical remedy.

Similarly, a stock swap with a larger competitor (or supplier) offers tax relief and, in some cases, creates stable income or dividends. In a stock swap, the buyer offers shares of the their existing company instead of cash or annual payments. However, the seller who accepts stock instead of cash as payment for his company accepts the potential hazard that the buyer's stock will lose value.

History is full of sad stories where the buyer's company lost dramatic value or failed. In a stock swap or any kind of installment sale, the seller must scrutinize the buyer's prospects for survival. If the buyer is unable to continue making payments, the seller's retirement plan can collapse in a heartbeat.

In a cash sale, the seller is free from the company's ongoing activity. In a stock swap, future management decisions, personnel, the economic climate, and tax changes all have the potential to disrupt the seller's value and retirement comfort. In a sense, the seller becomes dependent on factors beyond his control.

A large block of any one stock can be a dangerous thing. A large block of buyer's stock is especially dangerous for the reasons noted above. The solution is a diversified investment portfolio across a variety of economic sectors. Concentrated holdings, such as stocks in the buyer's company, are reduced over time and carefully staggered to decrease taxes. A good diversification plan will reinvest proceeds to preserve future buying power and growth. Simply put, it takes a comprehensive plan to reduce the seller's dependency on the buyer in a stock swap.

Of course, reducing a concentrated holding may not be as easy as it sounds. Retired small business owners may find it hard to heed investment warnings because of psychological and other factors. Many retirees hold concentrated stock positions for too long. Loyalty to a former company can be a costly mistake.

The challenges call for specialized knowledge. The skills needed to start and successfully operate a business are very different from those needed to transition into retirement. A lifetime of effort can be destroyed by a few bad financial decisions. Thoughtful planning with a knowledgeable accountant, attorney, and investment advisor can help a small business successfully survive the transition from owner to retiree.

Chapter 19

Technology Offers Great New Options For Investors

Every aspect of our lives is better in some way due to technology. Bill Gates is the world's wealthiest man because of the remarkable changes wrought by the personal computer. In medicine, from recordkeeping to surgical instruments, the computer brings speed, accuracy, and precision duplication. Research and diagnosis are enhanced, and many mundane chores are eliminated completely. By any medical measure, our lives are healthier, longer, and more enjoyable because of this miraculous electronic box. Through Microsoft Corporation, Bill Gates harnessed computer technology and made it usable. Similar to Marconi with radio waves or Edison with electricity, Gates brought computer power to the masses.

Technology Creates Change

As noted earlier, products and services used to be distributed through rigid channels. Companies controlled product availability, information, and every step of the buying process. You may have had a choice of stores, but you had to choose *some* store!

Where did consumers get detailed product information? Where did they go to buy an insurance policy? If they needed a loan, where did they borrow money? In the old days, consumers had little information and even less clout. Companies could charge premium prices because they horded carefully-guarded trade secrets.

Investors could choose *which* stockbroker but not *no* stockbroker. It was a fairly efficient system except for one thing: *Customers paid high prices for trading because they had to.* Every transaction required paying a necessary toll. For instance, sales commissions were often built into the price (mutual funds or insurance products), and lacking another alternative, consumers paid them. Since some premium was built into nearly every investment product or service, people silently bore the pain.

Technology Creates Power

Technology put power into the hands of consumers. In a world where quality information and terrific products are just a modem away, dinosaur companies find it hard to survive. Information premiums are no longer a necessary toll and consumers simply won't pay them.

Want an example of consumer power in action? Think how the travel industry has been transformed since airline flights, hotels, and rental cars became available over the internet. Powerful consumers now compare pricing and availability from the comfort of home 24/7. It's hard to deny the magnitude of these consumer-driven changes.

Charles Schwab changed the investment world in 1974. He created a consumer-oriented brokerage firm offering discount fees to knowledgeable investors. Schwab is a household name today, but thirty years ago, he rocked the investment world, thanks to communications technology and a consumer focus. The brokerage industry has never been the same.

Some political scientists and other experts argue that the Iron Curtain's fall was more technological than political. The general premise is that people can't be easily suppressed when satellites and computers beam images of world prosperity into their living rooms. Citizens won't sit still for poverty and brutal dictators while neighbors live in democracy and prosperity." Information can be a powerful tool.

Technology Creates Opportunity

Knowledgeable consumers are actually *good* for businesses, because they can spend less time educating them and more time helping them. Consumers routinely bring research — quality research — into the store with them. Fewer costs, fewer mistakes, fewer unhappy customers. *More profits.*

Despite dramatic changes in the travel and investment industries, there are still legions of people who don't want to research product information, preferring to seek professional advice and assistance. They want to work with a real live, knowledgeable industry professional.

Still, the fact that outside product information is *readily available* threatens many older methods of doing business. It's nearly impossible to sell an inferior product or charge an information premium in today's environment (though a *service* premium can be collected). Consumer information destroys companies with shoddy products and egregious profit margins.

We are living in a *transformed economy of knowledgeable and sophisticated consumers*, people who can uncover the history of product defects and whether complaints were resolved. These are consumers with the power of knowledge.

Technology Creates Profits

Consumers will always buy products and services *somewhere.* Companies that embrace the new reality will thrive. Companies that ignore it will perish. True, some old-fashioned predatory companies still exist, typically serving miniscule market niches, but their days of sustainable profits are numbered.

Consumers, fueled by information, rule the business world. Companies understanding this new technological truth will prosper.

Chapter 20

What Is An Annuity?

An annuity is a formal contract, usually issued by an insurance company, promising a certain payment stream. For a price, you can buy a specified stream of payments. You trade a lump sum — or in some cases, multiple payments — for a payment stream that could be for a specified number of years or your lifetime. It might also include the lifetime of a beneficiary as well, with the amount possibly being decreased when passed to the beneficiary.

Some confusion exists about the difference between annuity products and annuity payments. In financial terms, an annuity is a stream of loan payments. When people buy and sell mortgages, they are actually trading an annuity, but it's not the product created by an insurance company. When academics discuss the advantages of annuities in a retirement plan, they are discussing the stream of payments — not a particular insurance product. There is a broad inconsistency among annuity products, some of which are just plain awful, due to the costs, terms, and rates. That, however, is not an indictment of the concept of regular payments.

Issuers of annuities, whether an insurance company or a pension plan, must deal with a lot of uncertainty. Actuaries, who are mathematicians trained in specialized calculations, appraise how long the annuity purchaser (and/or beneficiary) might live based on age, gender, and other pertinent data. Once the duration of payments is calculated, the actuaries estimate the investment pool necessary to pay it. Today's expanded retirement lifespan can cause a lot of uncertainty.

To protect the issuer, actuaries need reliable estimates for both longevity and investment earnings. If they pay too much or too long, the issuer loses money. For a pension plan, this mistake means the sponsoring company must add more money to the plan. For an insurance company, the deficit is paid out of reserves or profits. Neither of these options is acceptable to firms issuing annuities, so actuaries must be conservative in making estimates.

What does this mean to you?

Since actuaries are employed by issuers of annuities to protect the company's profits, their estimates are necessarily based on the conservative end of a conservative spectrum of investment returns. That means from an income perspective, you can likely do better.

How?

First, by using a broader pool of investments for your portfolio. Second, whereas the actuary has to estimate the future today, you can adjust your portfolio as conditions change. Third, there's no need for you to build in a profit margin for insurance company profit.

In addition, any residual amounts accumulated may be passed on to your beneficiaries. Remember, most annuity products are exhausted after the annuitant (or annuitants) dies. Also, there is no surplus paid to the buyer when an actuary overestimates longevity or underestimates investment returns.

Here's another important consideration. An annuity's stream of payments is inflexible. Should an emergency or investment opportunity arise, you cannot interrupt the payment stream.

Another related point is that inflation wreaks havoc on long-term annuity payments. Think back to your salary in 1987. Could you live on that amount today? Now, leap ahead to 2027. How much will today's monthly annuity payment buy in tomorrow's world? For this reason, annuity products that don't include an annual cost of living adjustment (COLA) should be avoided. COLA will reduce early payments but add purchasing power value down the road.

Lastly, never buy an annuity product without comparing prices. Every insurance company uses their own actuaries and estimates, which can vary greatly at any point in time. Annuity buyers, especially those with larger sums to invest, should solicit quotations from several highly rated insurers. Most local insurance agents represent just one company, and I always recommend a second opinion before buying.

Conclusion

One legacy from my father is the coin bank collection he left behind. It's unique — truly one of a kind — and includes dozens of mid-century banks provided by banking institutions to customers. Some are simple, others elaborate. Most are made of metal and almost all contain a locking mechanism. Some have mechanical counters to track the amount of money.

One of my favorites looks like an old cash register and it counts as you add coins. Surprisingly, it has no lock or key. Instead, the magical cash drawer opens when you've saved ten dollars. Until then, you are flat out of luck!

Today, coin banks are a novelty item mainly reserved for children. But for savers in the early 20th century, they served a vital financial purpose: an accumulation of coins could buy a month's worth of groceries or furniture for the home. Those savings served as an emergency fund in event of sickness or misfortune. Ten dollars was a relative windfall in the days of my father and grandfather.

The coin banks are a wonderful reminder of a world that used to be. How things have changed today. A bank full of coins isn't good for much beyond a premium cup of coffee. Many of us abhor coins as nuisance, and millions of people don't use or carry cash at all. Debit, credit, and gift cards have almost completely replaced currency as an exchange medium in America.

Still, I love the old coin banks. They are historical artifacts from a bygone era. Once, they were an important part of family finance, even a lifesaver in some cases. Saved coins bought groceries, household goods, automobiles, and modest tuition payments for first generation college students. Family coins and family coin banks made a real difference.

Old ideas, noble and rewarding as they once were, aren't much help today. They don't fit today's new world that requires new tools and new ideas to prosper. Our grandparents and parents did what worked for them, but many of those ideas aren't as productive today.

One key to family financial success is to update antiquated ideas. It doesn't require a lot of effort or super intelligence. Most of the updates are fairly simple and many Americans have already accepted some of them. Most will make your life easier and more productive.

It's time to throw out old money ideas. Tomorrow is now.

Appendix

FIX IT Ideas

FIX IT: Price matters more than quality.

- ✓ Consider potential resale value in every major purchase. Check eBay or other auction sites for prices on the pre-owned version of what you want.
- ✓ Create a value matrix to decide between choices. Include factors like useful lifespan, cost of operation, maintenance expenses, and convenience.
- ✓ A great way to own quality items is to consider pre-owned or refurbished products. Many have warranties and no one but you will ever know.
- ✓ Compare prices. The internet makes it easy to shop for the best deal. Everything from electronics, automobiles, and hotel stays can and should be compared.

FIX IT: "Neither a borrower nor a lender be."

- ✓ Divide your outstanding debt into good and bad categories: long-term, low interest debt that can help you move forward (good), and short-term, high interest debt that offered convenience and instant gratification but saddled you with ongoing interest charges (bad).

- ✓ Create a plan to eliminate the bad debts.
- ✓ Stop making extra payments on the good debt. If necessary, use that extra money to pay down bad debt. Once paid off, use the extra money to invest in yourself.
- ✓ Shop for the best possible terms for good debt. Refinance your mortgage if rates have gone down and consolidate other good debts. You don't need to pay them off quickly, but you do need to lower the cost of borrowing when possible.

FIX IT: Banks are the best place for investing.

- ✓ Choose a convenient bank for the cash services you need. Most people today use payroll deposit, ATM machines, debit cards, on-line bill payment, and an inexpensive checking account for reserve cash.
- ✓ Eliminate duplicate accounts where possible.
- ✓ Do not use bank certificates for long-term investing. At best, they are a temporary savings vehicle that pays consistent, but lower, interest rates.

FIX IT: Don't place all your eggs in one basket.

- ✓ Check institutional safety for FDIC or SIPC coverage and make sure you understand the rules. Most investments held in a brokerage affiliate or trust department aren't covered by deposit insurance, but that doesn't mean they aren't safe. Get the rules in writing: I'm often surprised by the misinformation provided by bank, broker, or mutual fund employees.
- ✓ Consolidate old retirement plans, IRA accounts, and personal investing into a single, inexpensive, and convenient institution. Again, seek the services you need. Most firms offer free or almost free check writing, debit cards, ATM machines, and online bill paying.

FIX IT: Extra effort always yields extra results.

- ✓ Unless you are a stock market hobbyist, stop wasting time trying to outsmart the market.
- ✓ Choose where to productively invest your time. People spend hours studying *Consumer Reports* about new cars or washing machines, then spend thousands on a hot investment tip from their barber or hairdresser. Similarly, you can often get higher personal returns from a community college course than watching CNBC's *Power Lunch.*

- ✓ Delegate investment chores wherever possible. Consider letting utility companies and others automatically deduct monthly payments from your brokerage account. It saves me an hour each month that I used to waste writing checks.
- ✓ Let 401(k) and other monthly investments automatically buy a mix of mutual funds or a target date retirement fund. Review annually, but resist the temptation to adjust frequently. That's a time-suck that rarely adds value.

FIX IT: The stock market is a casino.

- ✓ Nobody has to gamble at investing unless they want to.
- ✓ Consider using lifecycle or target date retirement funds to assure broad diversification with professional management. Avoid individual stocks and any kind of hot tip, even those touted by the media.
- ✓ Stick with mainstream products and services. If the product or idea can't be found in a recent issue of *Money* magazine or *USA Today*, it is not for you. Don't gamble with family money.

FIX IT: Do-it-yourself is the best approach.

- ✓ DIY can be a fine way to save money if a task is simple and repetitive. It is not a good approach for complex tasks requiring customization. Yes, DIY for painting a wall, no DIY for custom ceramic tile in a large master bathroom!
- ✓ Every college savings or estate plan is customized and so is retirement investing. Don't try this without help. No matter how knowledgeable or smart, you can't possibly know all the nuances.
- ✓ Study the basics as a foundation for understanding financial products, strategies, and resources, but recognize the limitations of general information. Maybe you don't need to understand combustion engines to drive a car, but you do need to know how to steer and apply the brakes.
- ✓ Keep your knowledge base current. The world of finance is constantly evolving with new information, new products, and new economic environments. The more you understand, the better decisions you can make.
- ✓ Be an informed consumer in all things financial. A good advisor wants you to engage. In my experience, the worst clients are uninformed clients.

FIX IT: Advisors are for rich people.

- ✓ There are thousands of products, dozens of strategies, and nearly endless sources of information. None of these are customized for your situation.
- ✓ Avoid product-specific advisors, except for product-specific needs. Don't ask a banker to evaluate your investment portfolio or an insurance agent for estate planning. Instead, seek good general advice and then reach out to professionals as needed. Insurance is an important part of most family finances, and a competent insurance professional can be very helpful. Determine what expertise you need, then seek counsel.
- ✓ Separation of powers is a good thing. Wealthy families typically engage a variety of financial professionals, including an accountant, attorney, and insurance expert. But they also use a knowledgeable generalist to coordinate their advisory team and streamline financial activities. A team can offer expertise, solid insights, and powerful collaboration. In fact, mega-wealthy families often formalize this process through a family office concept.

CPSIA information can be obtained
at www.ICGtesting.com
Printed in the USA
LVOW11*1100141216
517234LV00001B/4/P

9 781506 903248